Olivia and Jack

Learn About

The

'Touch'

SHEENAM KHAN

This is a work of fiction. Names, characters, places, and incidents either are the product of the author's imagination or are used fictitiously. Any resemblance to actual persons, living or dead, events, or locales is entirely coincidental.

Copyright © 2025 by Sheenam khan
All rights reserved

No part of this book may be reproduced or used in any manner without the written permission of the copyright owner except for the use of quotations in a book review. For more information, mail at:
Authorsheenam@gmail.com

Illustration Courtesy: Canva

Contents

My Body My Rules

Our body has different beautiful parts. Some are *'okay'* to be touched by others while some are *'not okay'* to be touched by others.

The body parts that are *'okay'* to be touched include the parts that do not make us feel bad, sick in the tummy, scared or uncomfortable. We can also call them the **'safe zones'** of our body. These are our hands, feet, head and shoulders. People can touch them with our **consent**.

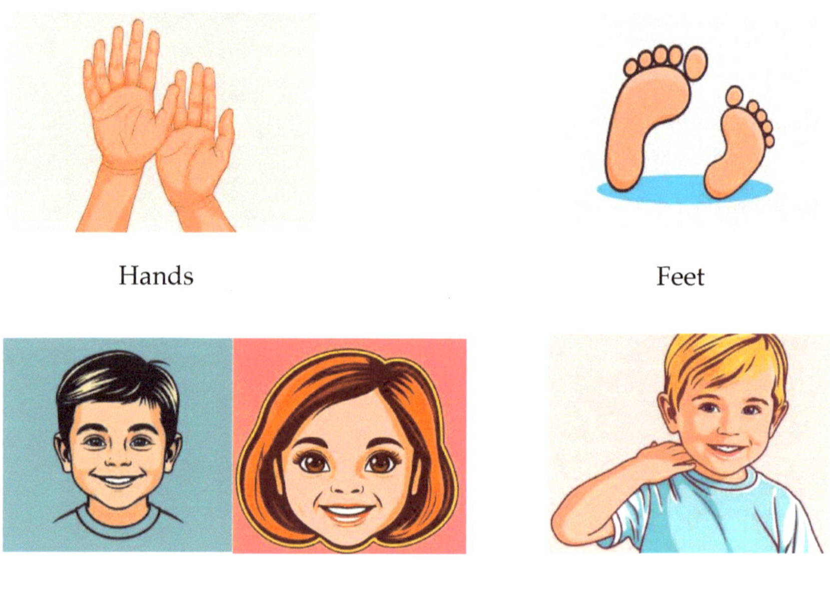

Hands　　　　　Feet

Head　　　　　Shoulders

Activity 1

Colour the given images and write the 'Safe Zones' of your body in the given boxes.

My Safe Zones

*I feel happy, secure and '**SAFE**' when people touch me on my 'safe zones' softly with love and care. However, not everyone is allowed to touch me even there. People whom I **like** and **allow** are the only ones to touch me at all.*

Now, lets talk about the '***unsafe zones***' of our body. They are our private parts that must never be touched by anyone regardless of our bond with them. They can only be seen or felt by us. These are our lips, chest, bottom and between the legs.

No one has the right to touch us on our '***unsafe zones***'.

Lips

Chest

Bottom

Between the legs

However, sometimes our parents or doctors may require to touch our private parts in order to check for injuries, infections or diseases. Parents can also help us change our clothes or washing our body.

In some cases, doctors may ask you undress for a detailed checkup. But if you are not comfortable to be checked alone by the doctor, you can always ask for it to be done in the presence of your parents.

A mother helping the child to change clothes

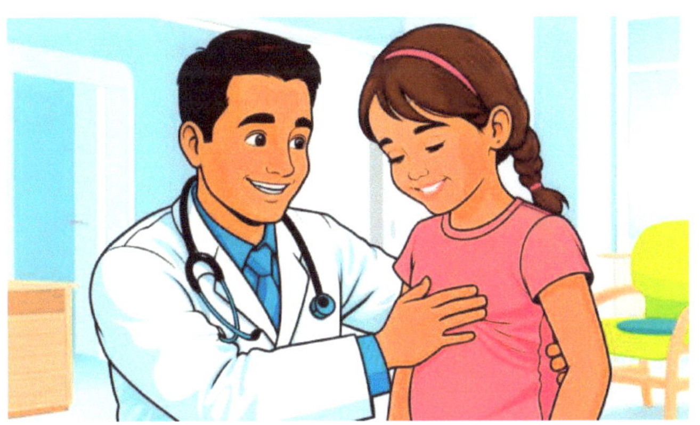

A doctor doing a check-up

Activity 2

Match the given body parts to their correct categories. One has been done for you.

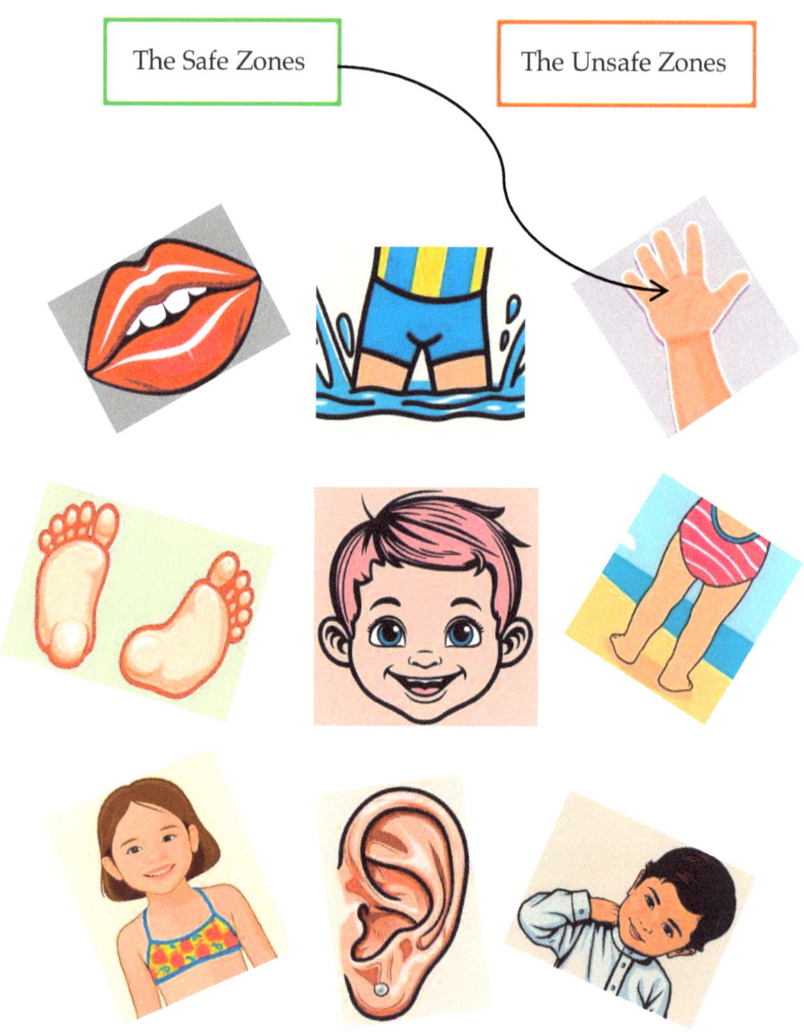

Good Touch

A good touch is any form of physical contact with the 'safe zones' of your body that makes you feel warm, happy, caressed and loved. A good touch must feel **'comfortable'** and respectful. It can be any of the following:

Shaking hands

Tickiling Feet

Patting Head

Wrapping arms against neck

Hugging

Kissing on the cheeks

Patting encouragingly on the back

Bad Touch

A bad touch is an unwanted or a forcible touch that is aimed at your private parts or 'unsafe zones' of the body. It makes you feel disgusted, angry, unsafe, disrespectful and above all, **'uncomfortable'**.

You should also be aware that a bad touch is not always aimed at your private parts but also can be on your body's 'safe zones'. But how can you distinguish the bad touch from the good one when it is on your 'safe zone'?

Well, the answer to that is, if a touch on your 'safe zones' feels hurtful, extremely tight and strong or abusive, it is a bad one.

REMEMBER

Bad touches can come even from the people very close to you, i.e., your family members like your uncles, aunts or cousins. Make sure to draw a line for closed ones too when it comes to your body.

Bad Touches on 'Safe Zones'

Squeezing hands

Pulling hair

Pushing hard

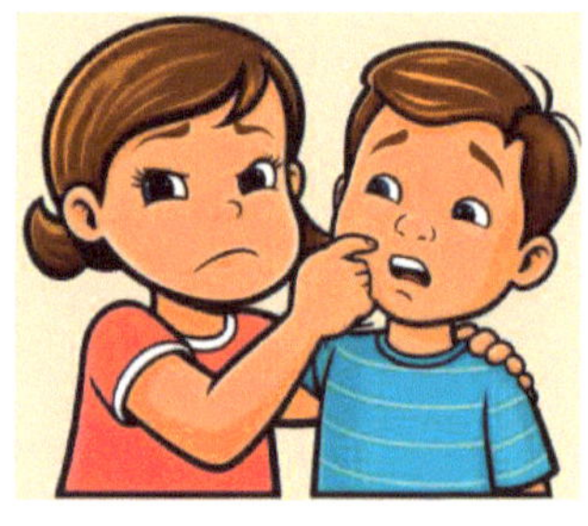

Pinching angrily or tightly

Tickling unwantingly

Kissing forcibly

Activity 3

Given below is a list of actions. Identify whether they are a good touch or a bad touch. Colour the flag GREEN if its a good one and RED if its a bad one.

(a) An ice cream seller touching your chest.

(b) Your grandpa kissing you on the cheeks.

(c) The security guard giving you a high five.

(d) Swimming coach holding your chest to
    save you from drowning.

(e) A young boy trying to hit you between
    the legs.

(f) Your cousin pinching your cheeks very hard.

(g) The teacher appreciating you by rubbing your back.

(h) Your classmate pressing your lips with her fingers.

(i) Your friends tickling you lightly in a game.

(j) The caretaker hitting on your bottoms.

What to Do When You Feel a Bad Touch?

Now that you know how to differentiate between a good and a bad touch, here is how you can react to both. While reacting to a good touch can be a subtle smile or a loving gesture, reacting to a bad touch needs much more power and intensity.

So, there are three things that you have to do when experiencing a bad touch by anyone. These are:

1. **Shout out 'NO'** - Scream at the top of your lungs saying **NO** or **STOP**.

2. **Run away from the person** - Get away from that person as soon as possible. If you can't run, then try to push him away from you and make noise to get others' attention. Try to get to your nearest safe place like school, home or a shop.

3. **Tell an adult you trust** - Finally, when you get to a safe place or get home, tell about the incident to the people you trust . They may be your mum, dad, grandparents, siblings or even your teacher.

Activity 4

Under given are some to-do-actions done by children while experiencing a bad touch. State whether they did correct by drawing a 😊 or wrong by drawing a 🙁

(a) A stranger was touching Alex's bottom but Alex kept quiet.

(b) Nia pushed her classmate when he was hugging her tight.

(c) Max complained to his teacher about the senior boy's forcible pulling of his cheek.

(d) Ellie didn't tell her mother about an old man who touched her between the legs as he warned her not to do that.

(e) Sarah shouted 'STOP' when her best friend was trying to kiss her on her lips.

My Safe Circle

Every child must have its 'safe circle'. A safe circle is a group of people, usually adults, whom a child trusts the most and can confide in them when needed. Mostly, a safe circle includes parents, grandparents, siblings, teachers or family doctors.

However, it is not necessary that a safe circle should be only restricted to your family. Neighbours, friends or caretakers can also be a part of it if a child is sure of their trust in them.

So children, whenever something or someone disgusts or scares you, you must immediately tell everything about it to any one belonging to your safe circle. **You should never keep any secret with them even if someone tells you to**.

Activity 5

Who is there in your safe circle? Paste the pictures of 5 people in your safe circle in the given space and write their relation with you in the boxes together. Make sure to share it with them too.

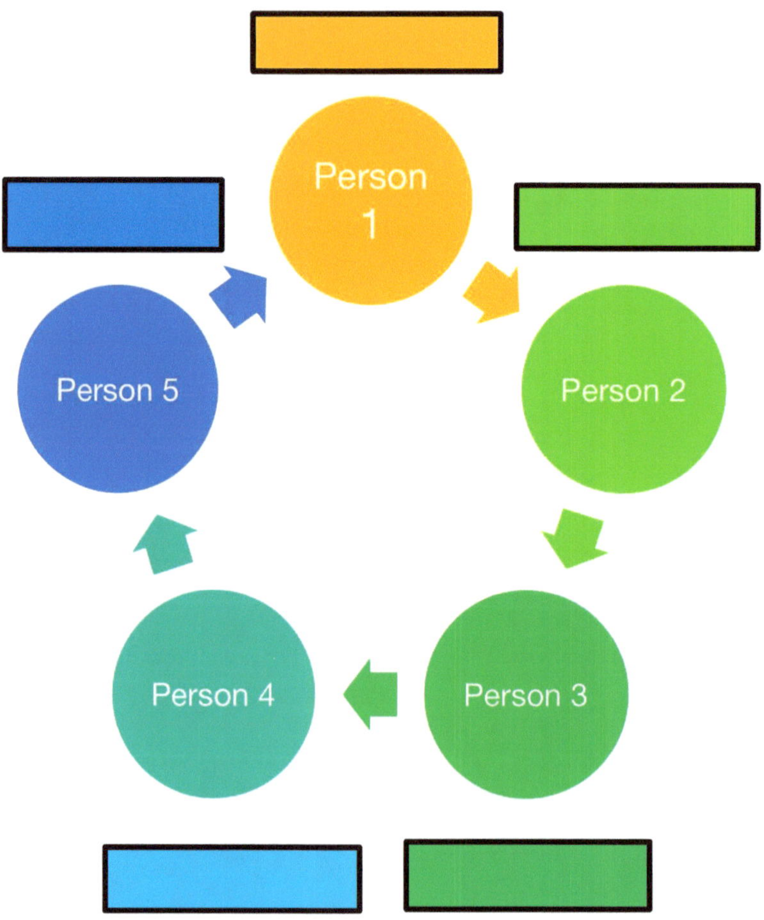

Meet the Twins

Olivia and Jack are twins. They study in grade 2 in different schools. Olivia studies in a co-educational school where both girls and boys study together while her brother Jack studies in an '*all boys*' school.

Hello! I am Olivia

Hello! I am Jack

They live with their mum and dad in a small house. And yes, they have a house help and a pet cat too!

Olivia Misses the Bus

One fine morning, Olivia got up late for school as she was studying late for her test the previous night. Mum was trying to get Olivia up else she would miss her school bus.

Olivia got up and rushed to the bathroom while Jack already left for his school. Olivia was still dressing up when her school bus arrived. It waited for 10 minutes before finally leaving Olivia behind.

Poor Olivia had a test that day. Her dad had left for his office. So, Olivia's mum asked her neighbour Mr. Maxwell to drop Olivia to the school as his office was nearby.

Uncle Max agreed and started his car with Olivia seated in the passenger's seat. After 5 minutes of the drive, uncle Max asked Olivia to sit on his lap as he found her too cute. He said to her, "Olivia, come on I am your uncle. Sit here and I will buy you an ice-cream on the way." Olivia agreed and sat on his lap as she thought he was close to her.

Then uncle Max started rubbing Olivia's cheek and hands which she didn't like. He then kissed her on cheeks very tightly. Olivia was very uncomfortable but she didn't say 'stop' though her body language explained all. When uncle Max understood that she was not happy with his touch, he stopped the car to buy Olivia her favourite ice-cream to distract her.

"Here you go! Now give uncle a kiss on cheek for that ice-cream." Olivia did as asked. Then she ran inside the school.

After returning home, Olivia said that she was very happy she missed the bus that day. Mum asked, "What was so special today Olivia? Did you enjoy going to school with uncle Max?" "Oh yes mum. He made me sit on his lap and he gave me an ice-cream. He also asked me to kiss his cheek for that. But mum he is very naughty. He was kissing my cheeks again and again very hard to annoy me."

"Olivia...when he was doing all that...did you like it? Were you feeling happy and comfortable?" asked mum. "No mum. I was removing his hands from me. I didn't like that. But he bought me my favourite ice-cream." said Olivia.

Olivia's mother understood what happened and said "Olivia, that was a 'bad touch' my child. If you feel bad or uncomfortable when someone touches you, it is not a good touch. Even if they are your family or friends. You should have said a big 'NO' to uncle Max when he was doing that. And remember, do not take anything from anyone when your parents are not around."

"Okay mum. You are right. I will scream 'STOP' if uncle Max or anyone does it again" said Olivia.

Mum never sent Olivia anywhere with uncle Max again or even around him alone.

Activity 6

Put a  on the things Olivia did right and ✖ on what Olivia did wrong that day.

Jack Goes to the Loo

Jack was waiting for the class to get over. He really wanted to go to the loo. After the teacher finished, he asked him for the permission.

When Jack entered the loo, he saw aunt Sally the caretaker, mopping the toilet floor. Jack was in a rush so he tried unbuttoning his pants but couldn't. When aunt Sally saw him struggling, she offered him help. As Jack couldn't control longer, he gave in.

While helping Jack unbuttoning, Aunt Sally touched him between the legs. He felt very sick in the tummy. "You were a little boy when you first came to this school in Kindergarten. Now look at you. You are growing into a big man really fast." said aunt Sally laughing. This comment added to Jack's shame and disrespect.

Jack asked her to leave the loo as he couldn't do his *business* in front of her. But she denied saying "I have seen you naked so many times when you were younger. Don't be ashamed of me." Now Jack got angry at her and shouted, "Please get out of here or I will complaint to my teacher. I am not comfortable to take off my pants in front of you"

Listening to his angry tone, aunt Sally left the loo quickly. When dad came home at night, Jack narrated the incident to him thinking he was rude to aunt Sally.

Dad said to him, "That's my boy! You did right Jack. Wash rooms are our personal space. No body can enter it without our permission. Not even me or your mum. I am glad you stood up for yourself."

Activity 7

A wash room is a personal space for everyone. You must decide your own rules when you are in there. Write 5 rules that you have set for your wash room trips.

RULE 1:

RULE 2:

RULE 3:

RULE 4:

RULE 5:

Olivia Comes Home Late

The school bell rang and Olivia came running to her school bus. All the kids were excited to go home. Amber got off at her stop so next was Olivia's stop as usual but instead of her, Bobby was dropped off.

Olivia asked Mr. Carl, the middle-aged bus assistant, "It was my turn not Bobby's Mr. Carl. Why did you not drop me?" "Today, we have changed the bus route due to a blockage dear Olivia. Don't worry, we'll be dropping you home at the last. Sorry for the minor inconvenience." said Mr. Carl.

Olivia never liked him. There was something about the way he behaved that made her feel sacred. Last week, she saw him threatening Natalia for something. Olivia sat back in her place. After all the kids were dropped off, Olivia was all alone. She felt thirsty so she drank water from her sipper but due to the rough movements of the bus, she spilled some of the water on her chest. Taking advantage of the event, Mr. Carl came running to her, took out a tissue from his pocket and started wiping the water off her chest very roughly.

After that he told her to take her shirt off as the water went inside which needed to be wiped too.

This time, Olivia knew that it was a **'bad touch'**. She instantly pushed his crusty hand away and shouted angrily, "Hey! Don't touch me. I don't like it. I can do it myself." Listening to her bold response, the driver shouted at Mr. Carl and he went back into his place.

Olivia was dropped at her home safely though late. When her mum asked her how she got too late, she told her everything that happened. Mum was so happy and proud of Olivia for escaping from a disgusting incident that might have happened.

The next day, mum went with Olivia to her school and narrated the actions of Mr. Carl to the principal. He was fired immediately as there were other parents too with the same complaints for the first time.

Olivia asked her mum, "Did I do the right thing mum?" "You did perfect my love!" replied mum.

Activity 8

Paste the pictures of your school bus or private driver, bus assistant, caretakers, and cleaners along with their names. You may ask your parents to take their pictures or you may find them in your school magazine.

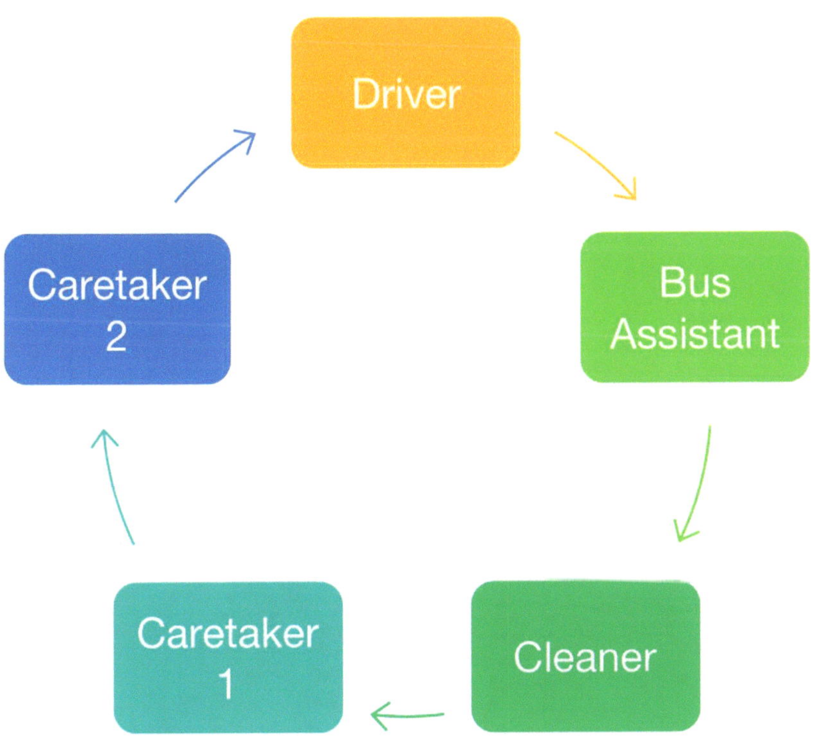

Jack Plays 'Tag'

Jack and his neighbourhood friend Stephen were playing tag in the public park near their home. Stephen's parents and his elder teen brother were also there. Jack and Stephen were having a great time. They were hitting each other lightly in a playful mood.

Stephen's brother Harry was a bully. He came to the park with his friends. They all saw Jack and Stephen playing peacefully so they decided to join them to have some 'fun'.

"Can we join you both in this game?" asked Harry. "Sure! So, shall we tell you the rules?" asked Jack innocently.

Harry and his friends laughed and said, "we make the rules kids and you follow them. Now come on, start running and if we catch you, we will smack your bottom." Jack and Stephen thought it to be a cool idea. They started running and soon were caught by Harry and his friends who hit them very hard on their bottoms. First, Jack tried to hold his tears to appear strong but this kept going on for a long time.

"Stop it! You are hurting me. Don't hit so hard. I don't like this game. I don't want to play it any more." said Jack. "Oh, you are a such a loser kiddo, big men don't cry like you. Bear it with grace." replied Harry. Jack continued for some more time in pain. Finally, he burst out in tears and Stephen got so angry at his brother.

Stephen went to his parents who were jogging in the same park. He narrated the incident to them. His parents rushed towards Jack and hugged him. They called Harry and his friends and shouted at them for their disgusting behaviour. They also made the boys apologize to Jack and Stephen.

After that, Harry and his friends left the park. Jack and Stephen were so happy to be all alone again. They resumed playing peacefully.

Activity 9

A 'bully' is a person who tries to harm others in anyway without any cause. He makes fun of people's weaknesses and think that is cool.

Bullying may first feel funny but slowly it turns into a hurtful and distasteful thing. We can feel it quickly because it gives us a 'bad feeling'.

Given below are some actions done by a boy. Identify whether it is bullying or not by writing YES or NO in the given boxes.

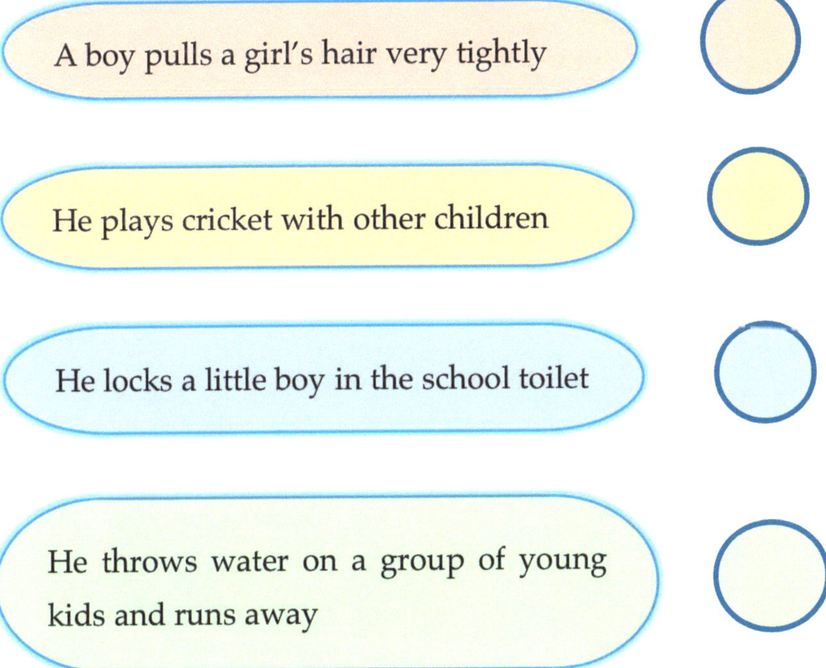

The Twins Meet Grandparents

It was time for Olivia and Jack to come back home from school. Both of them entered together at the same time. They got surprised and happy to see their grandparents sitting in the living room. Both of them rushed towards the grandparents and hugged them very tightly.

Olivia sat on grandpa's lap while Jack sat on grandma's. They were kissing their hands and showing love. The grandparents too were kissing their foreheads, cheeks and hands in response.

Both the twins were extremely comfortable and at peace with the grandparents' touch because they could feel the love, warmth, comfort and care in those touches. They didn't take a second to understand that it was a 'good touch'.

When mum asked them to change their school uniforms, they replied, "Grandma and grandpa will help change them today mum". This represented their comfortability and trust level with their grandparents.

The behaviour of Olivia and Jack shows us that a child knows if the touch is '**safe**'. If he feels good, he will respond to show that, otherwise we should know that he is not liking it and that it is causing any sort of discomfort to him even if it is from a very dear and near family member.

The twins spent their entire day around their grandparents and even wanted to sleep with them. They were delightful and excited to be with them.

Activity 10

A child's actions and behaviour tells us a lot about their inner feelings. Complete the sentences which show that Olivia and Jack felt 'SAFE' and 'HAPPY' around their grandparents by choosing the correct phrases from the box.

kissed their foreheads   surprised and happy

grandpa's lap, sat on grandma's   delightful, excited

their hands

their grandparents , school uniforms

to sleep

(a) They got ______________________ on seeing their grandparents.

(b) Olivia sat on ________________ while Jack ______________.

(c) Both of them kissed ______________________.

(d) The grandparents also ______________________ as a response.

(e) The twins wanted ________________ to change their ________________.

(f) They also wanted ______________ with them.

(g) They were __________ and __________ to be with their grandparents.

NOTE FOR PARENTS

Dear parents,

In the current world, it is more than necessary for you to make your child understand about the difference between a 'good touch' and a 'bad touch'. But, it is also important to understand the ways in which you can do that. This book aims at teaching your children about it in a subtle and interesting way. Make sure you read this book together with them and do all the activities too. During the activities, it is highly recommended that you engage them in it to try and ask if something bothers them.

Be safe and alert!

Happy Reading 😊

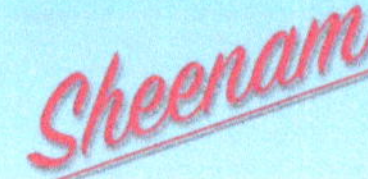